SONGS I'D SING.

songs i'd sing.

-marlo afton

oh, all the songs i'd sing,

if i wasn't a coward,

if i was a little bit louder,

a little bit tougher,

a little stronger to know what i feel,

and let myself think it was good and real,

but i never did.

i've been making up stories in my head since i was a kid,

and never thought i could say what was right, so tonight:

don't mind when my voice breaks,

or my hands start to shake,

i'm just trying to be brave,

do what you told me i could,

whatever i dreamed of, "darling, just make it good".

to all the special people who told me i
could.
thank you <3
-m

author's note:

hey, that's me! i'm marlo and i wrote this book. it's a collection of thoughts that i've had over the years and finally organized. my family and most of my friends could confirm that the majority of my teenage years were spent obsessing over music (taylor swift is mainly to blame), but not just listening. i analyzed, poring over word choices, and learning the backstory behind every song to understand where it was coming from. that honestly goes to show how amazing the human brain is, because i'm surprised there's still room for anything else after the hundreds of hours of lyrics i have committed to memory. i thought being able to write and create things like that was so awesome and wanted to try it and had always loved writing, so i did. the melodies never came as easy as the lyrics flowing out of my mind, so i gave up on this project a hundred times but kept coming back to it. writing these "songs" was a way for me to let out and understand what i was feeling when i didn't know how to explain it to anyone else. recording my feelings in these poems when i genuinely never knew whether they'd be read or not, was freeing in and of itself, because writing, and the feelings i was trying to explain through it, is something that's universal. in august, about 3 months ago, i decided i wanted to publish these thoughts and share what i loved and didn't want any of my other insecurities to hold me back. so, these are my experiences, my feelings and thoughts, unfinished majorly, but the songs i'd sing. a little journal of my heart, thanks for letting me share it with you :)

table of contents

love.

happy, glittery, and blush-y in the movies, biting your cheeks to keep from looking like a total fool, and feeling like your chest could burst at any moment for reasons contradicting your own self-preservation. also constantly having a twisty, jumpy heart and stomach, in the best way. platonically or romantically, your mind either has so many words to say you can't get them out in a way that justifies the feeling, or you don't feel like you need to say anything. both are completely unique and so wonderful and confusing. maybe most noteworthy, completely submitting yourself unselfishly to some-one who's not you, and being okay knowing that this could break you someday, but it's worth it. huh? absolutely crazy... I LOVE IT.

first.

i sometimes think i fall in love too easily,

trust with my heart but not my head.

because i fall for everyone i meet,

all while my head screams "not yet!"

up all night with butterflies, the lovesick kind,

but my mind holds me hostage from you,

because "it's all fake", "they'll just run away",

"besides, it's way too soon".

but i need you, want to be in your arms,

tell you my secrets, fears, and dreams while we lie in the dark,

but i won't-

because my head says so.

which is why inside's always a war zone,

constantly being torn apart

between what i think i know about love,

and what i feel deeper, our magnetic hearts-

it's tragic really.

but anyways, i can't complain, these types of things always make
the best art.

early summer

stargazing every night in june,

you say i'm always seeing shooting stars instead of you.

i've never been called lucky,

i don't think it's true,

it's just i'm in awe of the sky, and you stare at me, looking at the
moon.

but- don't move, don't slip,

right here's where i want to stay.

we could live a life like this,

every day would feel like a holiday.

you and i could be all we need if we choose,

we could take a shot and fight so we don't lose.

and when you ask me what i wish for while the stars streak
through the sky,

i sigh- and say "nothing", because i have you.

to stay

ever since i was little, i've thought running away sounded so romantic.

i wanted someone who could sweep me off my feet and take me places.

i'd talk late into the night on my bed,

joke about booking flights on the phone,

i wanted someone to run away with

because i didn't think i was strong enough to do it on my own.

but that's changed-

now, i want someone who will stay.

i think that's the bravest, most lovely way to show you care;

to walk into someone's life and say you'll be there,

and show it and stay.

for new jobs and rainstorms and first days

when you're scared to walk through the door,

but holding a hand makes it bearable.

to know when you get crushed and run over that at the end of the day, you can go home,

and that that home is in a soul.

i think that's love, and that's what i want.

home

you almost feel like home,

which is crazy because i've known home way longer than i've
known you,

but i think of warmth and safety, and your smile seeps into that
picture in my mind,

and your eyes bring the same comfort of my mom's warm dinners
at home on family nights,

and i can see you there

tangled up in our crazy hair forever.

memories- glowing golden and growing old through the kitchen
window.

you=home.

afternoon drives

sunlit stares,

your pretty hair that blends with mine

and golden eyes,

i want to smile, but i bite my cheek

because it's silly how happy you make me,

it feels like a secret i should keep,

but i think these are the happy moments

i'll look back on when i'm old

and you're five months older;

500 autumns wouldn't feel like enough

to get to do all that i want to with you,

but i can let that be,

if we can spend 70 more years together like we're still eighteen.

twin soul

this is hard for me to do, because i've never had anyone else like
you.

there's so much love and nothing to compare it to,

but i think God made us in the same thought

so someday we could find each other and help guide the other back
home.

i bet he smiled when we met,

two of his daughters who love so fiercely, they'd never felt the same
back from a friend.

i have lots of favorite parts about you,

like 5-minute voice memos sent when we can't sleep at 2,

collaborative playlists, and how our arms link perfectly,

so similar people assumed were sisters, or cousins, or something
alike,

which honestly, i really wish we could be,

but i'll settle for friends for life.

you're nice to the boys i introduce you to, even when you've heard
terrible things,

and answer my calls on the drive home, swallowing tears i didn't
want them to see.

you never make me feel stupid when i realize how i was blind,

just sit in the dark car for hours, be the person i need- to want to
know my mind.

i knew it was special when i didn't have to worry about coming off
too strong,

all the silly things i say, you just laugh along.

now i'm happier when i know you're doing fine

because somewhere along the way, your heart became connected to
mine.

i love you when we drive around town for ice cream,

buy beads we don't need,

and go home to watch tv shows that make our eyes close they're so
cringe-worthy.

take hours-long walks just for an excuse to talk,

explaining the details since we last spoke in a million little stories.

if it was someone else, the repetitiveness would get boring,

but you'll never do that for me

because somehow i think i'd be happy if you were my only friend,

and we ate at our lunch place every day,

ordering the same thing again and again.

i don't know if it was the way when we met the stars aligned,

i can't even remember the first day you became a part of my life,

but i know to just go on without you sounds like option #442.

i love it when we stay in and paint our nails and watch rom-coms,

but mostly, i love getting to sit there in each other's arms,

when the right now is heavy, and what we're reaching for seems so
far away,

and the people we want to love and miss are quiet, and nothing is
the same.

we can talk about it all or say nothing, but it doesn't matter,

because we have each other, souls made to be together in life and
after.

reason to stay

blue sunglasses on the counter,

strands of your hair left everywhere,

even my whole photo album of hours of smiles and your voice

couldn't make up for the hole of the silence when you're not there.

the way that your hands touch mine,

the way our eyes meet and, without moving, our mouths smile,

and the way you try to know my mind,

you're my favorite person born on this earth in a while.

i know you hate these talks, and when i get too serious without
cracking a dark joke,

but i'm so glad you're alive at the same time as i am.

so happy you're living and breathing alongside me,

that i can lay down beside you in matching hoodies and hear a
heartbeat,

i don't think i could make it through without you- if you weren't a part of my life.

don't hate me for ruining the mood,

but i don't think i'd love living as much as i do here with you,

and while i don't want to be the only reason you stay,

i'll let you hold on to it for now and forever if you need to.

i'll be here by your side if you're in the same universe,

i'll never let go as long as you keep up the fight, i'm yours forever and always.

your eyes

you find the flowers in the weeds,

you point out the green shoots among the charred black trees,

you smile and count to three,

because life's never as bad as it seems,

you show me the best parts of me.

you find beauty is in everything,

i find everything good in you; you're all i hope to be,

you say it's all there inside of me too,

i don't know how that's true,

but i want to borrow your eyes to see the world when mine get cloudy,

if you'll let me stick around,

teach me to see the beauty.

what would happen?

you and me,

middle school crush at 13,

say you've been trying for my heart since then,

you just never could find the key.

i laugh and blush because that sounds sweet,

you've always told a charming story.

been a few months of me feeling lucky,

but if this was a test, i'd still be the top reader,

because you haven't yet learned to see through me.

a little glad you can't tell i cried last night

thinking forward to the time you'll leave,

instead, i smile when i see you and say i'm happy,

because that's how i want you to remember me.

what would happen if you noticed the tears gleaming when i
turned away?

maybe we'll never know,

but i know i'd live lifetimes waiting for you to,

and maybe i will.

would you rather

playing "would you rather?' on the drive home,

under flashing lights, my eyes close:

i think i'd rather have the power to control time,

because then i could stop what i know is coming,

i could live here until i'm ready to leave,

keep your hand wrapped tightly around mine.

"would you rather die by ice or fire?",

i don't know, and it doesn't make a difference,

i think i'd rather die with you by my side,

but that doesn't matter, right.

i'm only playing this game for you,

which is how i know if that scenario were to come true,

it'd be you before me because i don't want to see you hurt,

or worse, if i looked into your eyes and saw that it didn't matter as
much as i needed it to.

but that's okay,

i settle and say probably ice,

you laugh and hold my hand, walk me to the front door and say
hanging out was nice,

i go inside, thinking of more questions and answers,

i'm glad you're probably asleep, because it's all just fun and games,
right?

it must be nice to not be in love, have your heart always be the one
on the line.

let you go=i love you

.   i never understood "if you love someone, let them go."

because i've always thought love meant staying and fighting and
holding on until the end,

but then there i was one day, biting my cheek to keep from saying
what i really feel

because i knew it would make it harder for you to leave

when that's what you needed to do.

so i sit here and bleed and watch you walk away, and it breaks me,
yes,

but i think there's no purer form of love

than hurting to protect a heart that's not yours,

and now, never will be.

romantic me

i want you to know that i still think of you fondly,

despite everything,

even when you found me whole and left me in two pieces,

i'm sure it's something you didn't mean.

the stories and warnings never tarnished you in my mind,

because i thought if i could love and be loved by you, it's all i'd ever
need to find.

i bet you meant well by pushing me aside,

you just wanted everyone to have some of your time,

and i still believe you were asleep that night

when i got a text from my friend who knew saying, "hey, i hope
you're doing alright…"

i always saw the good parts of you and wanted to make them a part
of me too,

when it fell apart, i still had faith you'd come home and find your
way.

i don't know why i'm writing this, knowing it's something you'll
never see,

maybe it's an alternative to the messages in your inbox that i know
you won't read,

but i guess if we ever cross paths again or my name comes up in
your mind,

you can know i'm on your side because i have been all this time.

i still think you're a good person deep down,

at least you mean to be.

i think you'd be a really good person to love,

you just weren't ever one to me.

loss.

confusing emptiness left after, no doubt, a lot of love. whether we realize it or not, everything we experience, every soul we love, leaves a mark on us, leaves us changed, and it can be hard to know what to feel and do once that living connection you were nurturing is dead. i think that "loss" is cloudy gray, churning, reeling, not sure where the way out is yet because nothing looks the same as it did before, but everything does; it takes you back to them. ha, yeah but remember there is no place for you there anymore, so turn around friend, you have to find the way out at some point. and it's okay if you take some of that hole with you, it really is a beautiful reminder of all the capacity you have in you to love someone else. if you did before, you can find it again, once you find your way out.

the same sky

it's been eight months since what i guess now was the last goodbye,

two separate lives, and tonight you're on my mind

while she's in your arms.

we're still under the same sky,

so, in a way, you were right when you told me we'd never fall
apart.

together in a way, i guess really anyone could be

if they're lonely enough and have a broken heart that still dreams.

summer boy

could've traveled to europe by now in gas money alone,

dollars i burned sneaking over to your home-

you never had time to text until at least 9:38,

my curfew was too early, and i sealed my fate by choosing you.

summer boy, we were golden until we were blue.

hours turned to days that i'd gone without seeing your face,

i called, but apparently, now the night was too late.

who were you turning into?

where did the boy i knew go,

the one who'd text me at 2

saying, "woke up thinking about you."

but i guess it's not june anymore- it's late july,

summer's slipping through my fingers despite all i tried,

it was just a moment in time.

your golden haze put me in a trance,

ever since that starry dirt road dance

forgot we were only temporary,

something that began with the end in sight.

take it or leave it

lay out my cards,

lay out my heart

at my last shot to get through to you,

but take it or leave it,

i bet you'll leave it,

then say you didn't mean it badly,

you just need some time for yourself,

i only wish you'd include me in your circle of help.

i could tell myself maybe you need some space, time alone,

the problem is i know you're still glued to your phone,

posting stories with your new friends, i'm not in them,

but you're in the back of my mind all the time,

now i hate the silence- it isn't right, is it?

how i predict your next move,

the new excuse,

the reason i was left behind,

the option you never want to choose

until you're alone

and way bored

and need someone to brag to,

and then i leave more hurt than before-why do i let you?

you leave me stone cold and empty,

but in a way that i can't help but crave you more,

like an addiction, only one that hasn't left me high in months.

one that takes the life away and leaves me alone and loveless.

it makes me feel sick- maybe i need help.

i guess you've turned us both into users:

using others to fill up on love you don't have was your part,

i just use you to abuse my heart.

in my head

in my head, i'm yours, still.

i still remember the weight of your hand,

my heart still beats, so i still feel.

i remember the rise of your chest when you fell asleep,

i remember being happy you felt safe with me,

i wanted to be your person and place forever.

i remember at the most inconvenient times,

my heart still holds you so close my head believes you're mine.

i've tried to forget, promised myself i will,

but i think it gets foggier because there was no end,

no break-up date or crazy fight,

at least if that happened, it'd give me something to laugh about,

instead of keep me up at night.

but in my head, you're maybe on a cruise,

a place where cell service can't reach you,

and any moment soon, you'll see my messages

and respond with how much i've been missed,

and i'll be so relieved to be done waiting because i was starting to
think it wasn't true.

more than skin deep

it's not just that i miss you,

physically near,

lying on your lap and you playing with my hair,

when i told you i felt sick,

and thought everything was happening too quick.

i don't only want to hold your hand when i feel like i'm slipping,

don't only wish i could collapse in your arms, the way you were
always willing,

i don't strictly miss kissing you and smiling without having to talk,

it's not just my body that misses you,

because that would be easy enough.

i feel you gone in my bones,

i miss you deep inside my soul,

which is so much worse and so much longer lasting,

because she knows things and remembers every time that's passed.

knows what i've survived, has feelings of what's to come,

remembers all my heartbeats and fast blinks and tears,

all the friends and lovers that have been a part of my life, a part of
me through the years,

and you're not leaving her ever- she knows you're here to stay

even though your feet are taking you on a different path a thousand
miles away.

i can't forget you because you were the peak,

the pinnacle of all i ever had been and thought i could be.

my skin will forget you

probably already has,

the way it sheds through every season,

her memory doesn't really last.

and even though i say i can feel you,

the outside shell i live in now never knew

what it was like to be held in your arms and blush under your view.

as years go by even my eyes won't be sure,

i'll admit, my mind has made your face more of a blur,

after all that i see, the new people every day,

i want to remember every outline, but i don't, and it hurts.

nothing is perfect at setting in stone, though i sometimes wish it was,

but i know you're not and never will be lost.

with me in the realest and most important, painful way,

deeper than things i can say or show i know,

i warned you a long time ago,

you're written in my soul.

let me be the villain

i think at once you knew i loved you,

i don't think you knew how much.

i'd explain to you now if you wanted,

but i don't want to open up that cut.

i'd be the villain in your story,

it seems that's all you ever wanted from me,

done trying to make it right- you already decided on the ending,

so i'll leave in the wake,

put back all the things i fixed just for them to re-break,

i'm tying back my own hands,

because i know if i don't they'll reach for you again.

so tell your stories, and i'll tell mine,

i hope it makes you happy; all the things you chose to leave behind,

walking off into the distance, i don't have to look to know you're
not coming after me,

but one last plea,

remember me

and my name, even though i know it'll never be the same.

i'll be your villain,

an old haunt, a silly fling,

paint me as any character you want,

anything to not be erased from your story.

cloudy skies

the rain drips and runs down my window

while i sit at the piano and look out

silently wondering if your skies are blue,

i want to ask, but i know there would be no answer,

and that's the strangest loss i thought i'd miss

the distance was expected when we crossed into different worlds,

but the small talk about the neighbors and the phone calls

with questions and big news that won't be picked up anymore, is
the wound that still hurts.

they've all told me things are better where you are, and that's fine,

but what's finer is the line i cross

between missing and resenting you for leaving me behind.

because i've been on my own for a few months now, learning again
to walk on my feet,

the new place i have to live in you never stepped foot in, and that's
when it hits me,

you were a part of the home i'm missing.

i don't know how to replicate what you were to me,

the comfort and the love and lessons,

i know the things i found in you weren't typical,

the way i could breathe in your understanding.

i guess this is just an empty i learn to live with,
a space i set aside,

to hold on and remember everything i memorized

from the last time i got to see your smiling eyes, hear your voice,
feel your embrace,

i thought i'd had to deal with heartbreak before,

but family is a lot harder thing to replace.

heartbreak either way

you said we'd always be under the same moon,

but does that still mean the same

if my heart's buried, left under the ground

and your head's in a different, far-away space?

and you said, "see you in 2 years", but it'll be more like three,

what'll i do if you decide to come after me?

because i love you but not enough,

it doesn't make sense to me.

i guess i never got the signal when one month got closer to three,

and our strictly platonic love got deeper, only i didn't fall for it,

i'm sorry-

but please don't make me say it out loud,

breaking more than one heart, like what jo said to laurie,
i was afraid that'd be you and me.

i knew it wasn't right that the last time we could've spent together i
stayed to watch that,

but i saw myself in that moment and felt her pain deeply.

i told you that night at 12:43 how i cried over that scene on the hill

i love you, but please find someone else.

i love you, but i will.

groundhog day

when i'm with you

i feel like i can't breathe,

i still haven't figured out whether you're the cure i've been search-
ing for

or the disease.

you break me when you leave,

then just as i find and recollect the pieces of me,

you're on my doorstep with a smile and a no-good plea.

i live in a state of "never know."

in the age of uncertainty, you make it so much worse,

every time i get back in your car, my mind forgets the hurt,

i forget what i want to be,

all to be the one who makes you happy,

it's sick.

i'm heartsick,

i'm homesick,

you do nothing to ease the pain,

you don't even notice the tears threatening to spill,

you just kiss me blindly because it's what you want,

and think of that- it's all you will.

because i'm out here stranded on an island,

you're the only lifeboat i see,

so i guess i'll keep falling for your fake rescue missions,

until the day you finally drown me.

~~the same~~

two diverging seas,

it gets clearer every time i'm with you, and the only one listening is
me.

i know who i am;

you know who you want to fit in with,

i know who i want and am going to be,

you know how to make others believe what you want them to see.

there's a big difference between those two things,

there's a big difference between you and me.

unfollowing

i wanted you to be mine so badly,

i spent my last summer crying,

every night i couldn't be with you felt like slowly dying,

thinking sometime you'd open your eyes, see that i'd been the one
to stay through it all,

that you'd choose me and make it all worth it.

i wanted you in my life so badly

that when i realized you weren't, i had to unfollow you.

online, in real life, it felt like there was no other way,

than changing how i drove home after work,

and stopping your posts from coming across because i know i
won't see us.

but just because there's one less person in your entourage, doesn't
mean my prayers for you are done,

i really do hope you're happy- just knowing you are would hurt too
much.

i have to imagine you disappeared, just a memory in time that's
gone by,

everything i can to erase you from my mind,

because the thought of you out there living life, one you never call
to tell me about,

one i'll never share and call half mine is too much.

if i'm ever going to be alive again, i have to unfollow,

stop asking for updates from my friends,

i think i'll make it out alright-

because last night you visited me in my dreams,

the first time i'd seen those eyes in 3 weeks,

caught me alone, and we danced, you pulled me in and said you
love me,

but i remembered and said, "no, you can't."

you faded away, and i woke up in a new reality,

me without you,

just me, a girl you never really knew.

missing the ex? (thanks to you)

he wouldn't have let a day pass without hearing from me,

and he would've held me on the porch step when i felt teary,

not only cared about me when i was cool in front of his friends,

he would've asked first to facetime every night,

and made sure i was happy and okay when i said i was,

and i wouldn't have to lay here and wish i had someone i didn't
have to swallow,

and smother and pretend my feelings didn't exist for.

he wouldn't be uncomfortable with the affection,

he would make me feel something if he was here,

even if when he left, that feeling was fear

that i'd never be enough for anyone else,

that i was a burden and crazy and would never measure up,

a mess, and lucky someone like him chose to love me because it
was work.

he would break me-but at least he cared enough to know it was his hands' work,

at least he held me tight and cut deep enough to leave this hurt,

at least i can see his bruises left on my skin,

and know there was a time when someone loved me "more".

the goodbye

haunted by the idea of what we once were,

some days, laying in my room, i think i hear your footsteps up to
my door,

you haven't been here in years, but i keep thinking you'll come back
because you never left,

not to me.

our goodbye wasn't final, no finish line to cross;

just waking up one day and seeing a hole where you were lost.

felt so permanent, but you're not so far,

sometimes feel like i could reach out in the dark

and your arms would be there again to hold me

and we could lie alone together and talk,

but i know you're so far gone-

you were for so long.

the whispers are still all around

of things i always wanted and words i didn't say.

maybe our goodbye wasn't final,

maybe it was just parting for now,

i hope i'll find out for sure in life,

but i know it won't be today.

aftermath

4 months and 14 days

since my phone screen showed your name,

you sent me a song about paris,

but now i'm embarrassed to see your parents.

we were a broken version of you, and a naïve me,

really thought that i'd found the long game, in my town at eigh-
teen...

now i need to make myself different so i dye my hair pink,

and you claim you can't see the night sky without thinking of me-

it's not that easy,

to get over, just forget what we were,

blocking my number won't erase us,

the new ones can't replace us.

you can see it in our faces,

there's no going back,

just a new you and me,

who we choose to become in the aftermath.

it's been long enough now that i shouldn't still miss you,

but my life, my heart grew around what i'd found,

and now that you've gone, there's a hole,

i'm like a tree without a home,

my ground moved without me,

but getting you back just isn't something i could ever do.

these days i see your eyes, not how they looked at mine, in campus
faces,

and don't take the long way home anymore because "those darn gas
prices"-

now it's 1am, we're lying in our beds feeling empty,

probably because we leave pieces of us behind in everything we've
loved,

once we felt fireworks and bright colors bursting,

but right now, it's as gray as your bedroom walls,

our hearts lie in pieces, mangled in the aftermath,

and our wounds stay open because it's not as easy to forget as we
pretend it is

when we pass each other's streets.

but that's just me-

learning how to live in the aftermath.

morning routine

i wake up to a blank screen,

breathe deep,

it's been 3 weeks.

i get out of bed to brush my teeth,

avoid my nightstand with the picture you gave me,

the one where we look happy,

and while i change into my clothes,

i change your name back in my phone,

take your name off my favorites list so i don't accidentally call,

remove your picture to trick my brain there wasn't an us.

7 months ago, we didn't know each other

and in 5 more you can say the same,

two separate people with combined- a thousand memories and
dreams,

back to strangers again.

the little things

tear-stained pillowcase in the morning

when i just did my laundry yesterday,

it's the little things left over from you that still haunt me.

i turned the heater on this morning, and the smell reminds me of
winter, reminds me of you,

when you'd pick me up almost every night and dreaded it, but had
me home by curfew.

i dyed my hair pink again because subconsciously,

i think i missed how i was when you loved me,

the smell used to be my favorite, like summer and honey,

but now it keeps getting in my brain and i can't sleep

because if i recreate the way i looked back then,

should you be calling saying you're on the way to me?

but it's been two months since we last spoke, which was really fine
until yesterday,

and i'm busy on my own, turns out you were right,

the college guys are cool, i'm talking to five,

and they make me realize i don't miss who you are now,

you weren't really that nice to me,

even though i loved you incessantly, and now i wonder how.

i'm okay until i see an email about sales for plane tickets and think i
should reach out,

it's only a second, and i feel stupid, but it gets me down,

because i realize that you're not around,

and now i have to find someone else to do the things i wanted to
do with you,

and because of the past i don't know if i can find anyone who will
like me enough for that.

i don't remember if you hate me or why,

it feels like i've been living in a dream since that last night,

because i told myself i wouldn't be sad when i just wanted to cry, and i've been distracting myself impressively well since then,

up here on my own, i honestly do love my life,

the words that i'm over you i've pretty much convinced everyone
are true,

i'm really fine 90% of the time, it's just the little things that still
haunt me about you.

it's easy

loving you is one of the simplest things i've had to do,

it's like just moments after we first met i thought "i won't forget you",

(or it'll take a long time for that to ever come true).

it's like i think of you as much as i think of me,

i wonder what you're doing while i'm brushing my teeth,

i'm so glad i'll be the one to tell you happy birthday on your 19th,

and hopefully at 83.

loving you is a difficult thing to do when it's been 6 months,

and i can't remember if you ever said i was something you love.

loving you really hurts to do because i remember every little thing:

how you smiled the first night under the stars,

the notes your voice cracks at when you sing,

but your mind doesn't remind you to text me back,

or that my birthday's the eighth of november.

after everything i've done to put you first i'm not special;

you don't remember anything.

not loving you is a simple thing to *say* i'll do,

when i promise my sister, this is the "last time" i put you first,

it's nothing personal, she just doesn't like me hurt.

it's easy to tell my mom not to get me wrong,

promise things won't go back to how they were,

you're just my friend first,

you don't have control over her strong girl,

and this time i won't let myself be forgotten on the side of the road.

it's easy to repeat the words that that was the last time i love you
and get left behind

when my eyes are so cried out, they're green,

maybe if i say it enough out loud it'll be true,

maybe i'll be able to want to get off the floor,

look at myself and see me for more than every reason i wasn't enough for you.

my most repeated lie is that it's easy to not love you.

au revoir

bite my tongue, taste the blood,

i just wish you were the one,

wish it wasn't "just for fun" for you.

mom said, "when you love someone just say it",

dad said, "if it's real he wouldn't have to fake it",

i hate feeling like i'm tempering my feelings for you-

because i love you and i'd be patient,

i like you standing next to me and want you to stay,

but i don't think it's my place, my right to say.

"love someone, let them go",

doesn't feel right to my soul,

i don't want to be the first one to lose my hold in this silent war.

for you to love me, i'd wait ages,

be proud still loving you when i'm ancient,

won't say your name, you know who you are,

the reason i learned to play guitar,

but i can't live feeling out of control,

because when i ask you never know.

drowning under waves of words we'll never say,

tired of "just friends" that act like lovers,

two kids who can't figure out how to love each other.

my sister told me, "know your worth", "he's not a man, just a boy
jerk",

all i hear is folklore that the right one's out there and this will all be
worth it,

i want it to be true, but somehow i still see him being you-because i love you and i'd be patient,

the way your hand holds mine just feels so right,

but no matter how strong i feel, i know it'll never be the night.

i know, and i knew then, and i've known,

which makes it embarrassing, don't want anyone to see

how hard i've tried to keep you here, doing life with me,

and it's all about you all the time, which is fine

until it's not, and now i'm tired,

but you should know-

for you to love me, i waited ages,

would've been proud still loving you when i was ancient,

mr. "no deep talks", you know who you are,

the reason i taught myself guitar.

if you ever know, just let me know,

but for now, i say "au revoir" instead of "a bientot".

remembering

for the sentimental, nostalgic part of you (approximately 100% of me). memories are the coolest things- pieces of life and moments your brain chooses to hold on to, and preserve somehow for when you need it, for better or worse.

another life

i tried to speak my mind,

but the words never came out right.

they got lost in the translation,

your interpretations never matching the depth i thought i saw
behind your eyes.

like a candle, we flickered away,

getting dimmer day by day,

i did everything i could to freeze the picture, make you stay,

all the efforts were in vain,

"us" a memory past, blown out with the wind as the seasons
changed.

so i say goodbye, knowing i'll always care for you,

maybe in an alternate world, another lifetime,

loving each other will be something we'll both be strong enough to
do.

i miss you, stranger

i miss you,

and i don't even know where you are,

i need you here in my arms,

the soulmate i haven't met yet,

at least not in this life,

but i can feel our souls are tied

and i long for you-

hope i can meet you again soon.

visitor

i saw you in my dreams last week,

your hands were tan and callused,

your eyes were the same hazel gray-green,

the ones that mixed with grandma's brown and got passed down to
me.

you came and spoke in a voice i used to know and laugh at,

i hadn't heard it since 2015.

you must've known i'd been feeling lost,

because you held my hand and said to keep going,

you promised me i was on the way to big things,

that there was a work saved for me, and i'd be able to do it with the
right team.

i've always believed everything about you,

the stories, the way you lived with giving and integrity,

everything you were, i want to hold up,

i frequently think of your name, how there's a lot to live up to in
that legacy.

i woke up from the dream i hadn't known i was in,

my room looked the same, but things had changed.

i forgot you weren't still here,

it didn't feel like a dream,

and even though you're not anymore, your words still help me
believe.

7 years of distance had been so long, and i know what real life
would say,

"ghosts", and "delusional", and "crazy", they'd take it in a cynical
way.

i can't explain it, my brain wouldn't know how to defend what i
felt,

but until we meet again,

and your smile is something i can picture, more than just a
memory,

until i can next hear you call our name, thank you for spending the
night with me.

i still find you

i live through loving things.

which is why when you left me i felt empty,

because i didn't know what life could mean

if you weren't what i saw in everything.

when i stopped hearing you in my music,

and breathing you in the nighttime breeze,

when i stopped feeling you in the sun and smiles and hugs,

and thinking of you in the most menial things,

it went gray.

but time still passed, and you faded into not a person anymore, but memories.

i get glimpses and flashes in my morning commute,

the streaks of colors in the sky that make me smile, even on cold nights,

the laughter i hear when i walk through the park,

lovers on the pier watching the sky get dark,

the patterns of the birds and the dance of the bees:

in them i find you; you're still with me.

write me a letter

write me a letter,

seal your love in an envelope,

so i can have some part to hold,

when i don't know your heart anymore.

write me a letter,

i swear i'll keep it forever,

it doesn't matter if you don't think we'll be together,

in 5 years or 20, for worse and for better.

just leave me with a footnote,

a physical memory,

of times you and i were a "we".
i'll smile when i see it,

keep it in my doc's shoebox,

maybe i'll even read it on quiet nights

to remember i'm alive,

that i mattered in someone's eyes,

enough to keep a record,

my favorite kind of treasures.

please write me a letter before you leave,

so i can carry a little piece of you with me.

10 years

my favorite blonde since 2012,

every teacher we had wouldn't put us together,

because they knew we were already best friends, an unspoken pact
for forever.

we were going to be bridesmaids at each other's weddings before
we even liked guys,

those days all we wanted to do was play in the dirt and shave our
heads bald,

what a time- to be nine.

i remember you showing me into the new school, which was nice
because i was shy,

sat by me through multiplication tables, under an inspection of
new eyes.

walked with me to the bus stop when the sun was barely coming
up,

and taught me how to swing on the playground, which i'd never
done,

you were the first and closest thing i had to a best friend who was my age, and a girl.

even when months went by in high school, busy with sports and work,

the years of memories bound us so that the time passed felt like none at all,

bike rides every 4th-grade morning, staying up scared together camping,

football games, boys we'd hate, and bracelets we'll keep forever.

through double dates, and same-timed breakups,

i'm glad i have you as my safe space,

a vault where we can share our fears and things that still hurt after a year,

and drive past our exes' houses, screaming songs out the window.

i miss hanging out with you on that famous dirt road,

watching the same movies, hiding under backseats, and laughing about everything.

now we're in different places, and our porch talks over the phone, we catch up on people and places the other doesn't really know,

but it's okay because i know the little girls we were are still the
same,

just more grown up and pretty, with bigger things on our plates.

but know you'll still be my bridesmaid, whether it's to s, or m, or j,

or some other letter that i don't yet know the name,

our kids will grow up buddies too, we'll be the favorite honorary
aunts,

and let's still be neighbors at our summer homes on the coast,

because living a movie life with you is one of the daydreams i visit
the most.

your eyes and smile first made me feel like i belonged,

funny, loyal, smart, protective, and everything in between,

from 2012 through the decades, you hold on tighter than the trend
of skinny jeans.

thanks for listening to my dreams, my rants, and life plans,

for sharing m&m's, secrets, and baby names, taylor swift album
release nights and texting until 3,

thank you for being my best friend through everything.

you're here

i still save the big cookie pieces

in our favorite brand of ice cream,

even though the next time you visit, i'll probably be 19,

which seemed so old when we were 8 and 4,

playing old in our backyard treehouse,

now we just talk over the phone when we're bored.

they say the distance makes us far away;

no, you're not here in my apartment,

but know, you are here in my heart.

i still think of you every time i step over lines,

how counting the sidewalk cracks our scooters rolled over was our
favorite pastime.

i wonder if your autumn afternoons are half as fun this year with-
out me,

which sounds selfish, but it's only because mine aren't.

laying in the grass under trees looks more lonely,

and spinning 'til i'm dizzy just makes me look crazy,

but i do it on campus anyway,

because you taught me life's more fun when you're not afraid

of what people wish they could be, what they miss about being kids
like us.

no, we're not in the same place geographically,

but know, we'll always be that close in my heart.

to my backbone

my support for the last 18 years of life,

my guidebook through math, friends-turned-mean-girls, guys that
i like,

you painted my nails to stop me from biting,

and held me in your lap when i failed to keep from crying.

i did some stupid things in winter you lovingly told me weren't
right,

you showed me paths to fix it and forgive, always on my side.

you told me how i'm special and deserve to be loved someday,

that even though i was tired and doubting, to keep going and keep
faith.

you kept most of my drawings, letters from when i was eight,

let me infiltrate the car bluetooth with my music, told me my
passions were cool and great.

i'll never forget you looking out for me,

making sure i was safe and fighting when i was weak.

you're my coolest, longest friend,

and even though we're not under the same roof, i know that won't end,

because once the questions were about calc, spelling, and high school dating,

now i call you about my latest dreams, business ideas, and recipes i need.

after a few years and a few more guys' names to learn, i bet it'll be a different query,

and even more so in the next decade, because i'll be wanting to be more like you,

raise them the way you did me,

when i wasn't paying attention, too busy complaining.

but you'll probably just tell me i can't mess up

because something you've always been good at is believing.

thank you for holding me up when i can't yet on my own,

when i'm weak and scared and unsure,

thank you for standing beside me every time,

thank you for still trying to shield me from the wolves,

even when i think i'm too old,

thank you for being my backbone.

8 feet tall

i used to think you were 8 feet tall,

you were a giant in my eyes.

the way you'd hoist me on your shoulders through costco,

and knew the answer to every question burning in my little mind.

everyone told me i looked just like dad,

i thought for sure it was the eyes,

i never minded being your little buddy,

tagging along to camps pretending i was "one of the guys".

you always made me feel wanted as your daughter,

showing me to everyone like you'd never seen better.

you taught me to share food and talents,

learn strangers' stories and remember names,

you cheered through all of my swim meets,

late and worn from work but still, you always came.

from you i learned cats are evil, dogs are good, and ice cream is
always right,

that people are better than you think they are,

and to never leave my sisters behind.

they're my greatest friends now thanks to you, just like you're my
favorite guy.

you showed me the meaning of brave,

you were strength when i wanted to quit.

you taught me "i can't" isn't real,

but you never minded when i'd cry to feel.

now that i'm older, i see you're more like 5'10",

and your eyes tear up a lot more than i used to see,

like when you finally gave in to watching one of my favorite
movies about a city of stars,

i think it's sweet, i'm glad you taught me how to have a soft heart.

you're still so much stronger, in faith, in strength, in scars,

i know if i ever needed it, you'd still carry me in your arms.

these days whenever i say my name and i'm associated with you,

i want more than ever for people to see parts that are the same
between us two.

i want to be told i have your eyes,

not just because they're beautiful, but because they're kind,

because they look for things that most people don't find.

i want to be told i have your smile, your laugh, your hugs,

that make everyone feel welcome and loved, and like they belong.

no matter how big i get,

i'll look up to you with big hazel eyes,

maybe not 3 feet taller, but someone i'll always be trying to reach,

your little girl forever from now, since 2003.

please remember my name

in a few weeks moving to a place where no one cares about my
name,

but you told me even if that's true you'll still tell my stories a few
states away.

i think that's sweet because i'm really not that special;

wish i could have one moment to not be miss sentimental.

cried every night this week lying in my bedroom,

because the night when it'll be the last as a kid is coming too soon,

i've outgrown here but i haven't outgrown you-

so please remember my name,

even when it's not the same,

even though i'll miss some family dinners

and my sister's birthday.

please remember my name,

how i'm grateful for everything you gave,

and i miss your face,

and even though i left i still need you in my life the same,

so please remember my name.

know i'm probably teary in my dorm room

on the nights when i don't call you

because i want you to know that i'm fine,

don't worry you raised me right,

gave me the best life,

you'd tell me i can do this tonight.

i've always believed your words are true,

and i love you,

so please don't forget me when i'm gone.

i'll be back before too long.

we can drive around and listen to all our songs,

stay up all night watching our favorite movies,

and catch frogs out by the pond.

we'll be different but for a little we can pretend it's the same,

just please remember my name.

alternate ending

i was thinking about us the other day,

the memories and plans and favorite movies,

sometimes i feel silly for all that never came,

but i've decided if the time comes, i'll tell my kids about it someday.

if you keep our pictures, i hope you'll tell them my name.

maybe if there's no way you ever let them see my face,

at least tell our stories if they ask.

don't forget all the good times we had as two kids learning to love,

i think it's a good lesson, that even though it ended with hearts in
some pain,

we both made it out and made lives that are still great,

and while the girl i was will always love you even though our story
didn't end in a typical way,

we aren't forever stained by the past, just changed,

because the end of the world is really the beginning of the good
stories to unfold,

you just can't see that yet when you're eighteen.

growing

changing. the most painful part of life sometimes, but the most beautiful and my favorite, because every day you get to beat the odds and realize that life goes on, and so do you, even after everything.

habitual

just like visiting home and opening up old drawers,

when there's nothing for me left from before,

someday i'll stop going back to you,

opening that door only brings back hurt

and disappointment for all i thought we once were,

but this is a part of me i can fix.

i'll find someplace else to place my love and talents and late-night
talks,

i'll find some other route home;

you are a habit i can break too.

1:11 wakeup call

1:11 on the alarm clock,

i couldn't stay in my dreams tonight,

can't turn off the buzz in my mind.

the lightning flashes through the dark,

the steady beats of thunder start,

i always told you i liked night rains best,

so, this feels like a blessing i would've missed if not for the unrest.

at night the storms hit hardest,

the desert: i guess she's a lot like me,

and this is the quietest my mind's been in any normal hours
since you and i were "normal".

and now the tossing and turning isn't me,

she covers my teardrops with her own and muffles shaky sobs,

and the pink-purple sunrise clouds in the morning tell me i can
paint over the darkness too,

make beauty after being the deepest black and blue,

calm and quiet where there was violence,

and light where there was fear and strikes of pain.

won't be long before i'm glowing again.

for me this time

feeling heartbroken and alone

is much worse when i'm not even home anymore.

i want to cry but i'm in a foreign place

where i have to function because the new life i'm trying to find
doesn't take a break.

calls to mom will have to be enough, even though i can't feel her
hugs through the phone,

because it's been a month and i guess i'm ready enough,

being split in half will have to do,

because i'm not who i thought i'd be,

but i guess i have to find who that person is without you.

i'll have to remember who i was before

i fell in love with something i never really understood,

rewrite the narrative, rewire my brain,

remember who i was before i changed in a million different ways,

trying to evaluate which girl would be the one you thought was
okay.

but no matter what i did, the oceans crossed, the bridges built, it
wasn't enough.

i hope one of these days i'll have enough energy to start building
worlds for me,

use my hands that held you and eyes that the good can see,
maybe that was just training,

building up endurance and strength to realize what i really could
be,

when i'm not building for you at the cost of breaking myself down.

what will i do without those constraints, all the pressure and ache?

i guess we'll have to wait and see.

a poem from someone wiser than me

a heart of gold gets heavy to hold

when there's no one to share it with,

a mind that writes in poems isn't understood

when no one else speaks the same language,

and you darling won't feel held here,

it isn't home anymore.

when you outgrow your pots, you find different soil,

i know it's difficult, but you have to keep going.

the journey is the only way to find where's right, the people who
are worth knowing,

to find a place where your heart fits, where someone will choose
you first

because of what they believe is under the surface,

a place your words will be searched for and understood,

where your love and intense need to care isn't seen as heavy and
crazy,

but something to live for, something needed, something good.

it exists, and somewhere in the future, so do you,

with a hand that's held in one who cares for your mind, body, and
soul,

a dinner table where you're invited and valued,

can share your dreams with those who'd fight for you,

and leave feeling as extraordinary as you are, and warm,

instead of alienated and silenced and cold

for things you've learned about yourself and the world others don't
know yet.

go leave here and find it, i need you to,

because somewhere out there is a little kid who feels the same,

and you need to show her the way,

that love and passion is real and true,

follow it, keep searching to find the place that was made for you.

stay starry.

i've heard people say it's too girlish to still wear flowers in your
hair,

a waste of time to wish on stars and watch the clouds for hours,
just to stare,

that it's childish to have a dream hung up on your tiny apartment
wall,

silly making plans to travel the world with no other ambitions, the
state of the world and all

but i don't believe them.

i think it's strong

and brave to do what you can to stay soft,

and think the world is beautiful and pure.

it is if you decide so.

keep wishing on butterfly wings

and kissing when you see 11:11

and giggling at the pretty simple things all around.

you're proving them wrong as you live,

because you know the truth,

after and through pain is the most beauty found.

a new season of me

life changes: we never stay the same,

sometimes the only thing i recognize about myself is my name.

i'm scared for the day, if you were to see me here again,

because i'm not the girl you left behind

and even i haven't decided if that's okay to say.

i don't think i could hold it together if you met my eyes

because i'd replay senior year winter nights

and feel like a fraud within my own bones

and that's not fair, so until i can get enough of a headstart,

please stay far away.

on my own

last i heard you went away to montreal or someplace like that,

what you're doing there frankly escaped my mind and i bet

if i knew that 3 years ago i'd die, because you were my life.

but now i'm at university, studying concepts so foreign to me,

and sometimes looking out the window my mind trails to think of
traces left behind,

there's not a lot there because you stayed painfully carefully on
your side of the line,

to the point where all i can do is laugh about the memories and
used to be's and staying up til 3,

talking to you and praying to heaven you were the one for me,

but turns out it's okay you aren't, because i'm studying at a big
college

and spend weekends exploring the dives in the city,

and smiling at the lovers and fall colors

because it turns out everything is so pretty,

even without you standing beside me.

i was vs. i am

i was vs i am,

a battle frequently fought in my head

when i want to move on but i remember all that i did,

when i'm trying to become better but then i see me, who i've been.

i was 17,

i wasn't picked first,

i am older now.

i know that i can't be everyone's favorite choice,

i am learning that doesn't lessen my worth.

i was treating perfect like the only option,

trapped by my own anxiety,

i am now allowed to learn from mistakes,

i can still feel anxious, but it doesn't define me.

i was unkind when i could've stayed quiet,

i hated myself for weeks,

i was wrong, i had help for the weight to be taken off,

i can give others grace the way it was offered to me.

i was used for my kindness, taken for a fool,

i sat and stayed quiet, believing it was something i did,

i gave you permission, i deserved to live feeling like this.

i know those were lies.

i am using those gifts to not harm myself now,

i am loving those who choose me in their lives.

i was "shy" for being thoughtful and quiet,

felt shamed for not spilling myself with the crowd,

but now i am living a peaceful life,

liking myself for the time i spend with the wind and the trees and
my mind,

and the people who appreciate that i keep close by my side.

i was hiding what i thought was cool if it wasn't the popular thing
in the room,

whatever was going on with them was my favorite thing too.

i am now proud to say what i love,

maybe i won't be everyone's everything,

but i can know if you say you like me, it's something you mean.

i was living life for you, who you thought i should be,

terrified to make a misstep,

overthinking every outcome,

doing only what i knew would be looked upon and approved,

i was alive but nothing left was mine.

i am living life as my own now,

the past left in the past, i'm going through each day presently.

i am loved,

i am free,

i am smart, kind and brave,

i am happy,

i am blessed with so much,

i am whole as who He made me, and who He's helping me be.

finally free

i'm trying to change,

but these chains i'm living with make it really hard to do

when for the past 7 months,

the only thing i was certain i wanted for me was you.

relying on someone human is a difficult thing to do-

it's harder when you weren't ready but i was set on making you.

i'm loosening what's holding me back,

i'm changing the way i see my past.

every day is a process, but i'm letting myself believe

that just because i didn't win you doesn't mean i'll lose at every-
thing.

it's okay that i haven't found something that's certain to stay at
eighteen,

because even though i stopped growing at 5'2",

everything about who i am is still changing,

and i need space free of waiting on you to know all that i can be.

it's not your fault that i finally saw i need to leave,

what you did with my heart just helped me hear and see

the things that i can do better to love and care for me.

maybe someday you'll come back,

and if you do, i'll be happy

because all that love helped me forgive you,

i already swam that sea.

so i'm determined if you find yourself,

find your way back to me,

either as someone who's grown and is ready to make space and give
up parts,

or as someone else entirely,

i know that will be okay

because as much faith as i had in you,

i have more in someone bigger than me,

and every day He's helping me change from the girl i was

when i let His creation be run over and used up and stolen,

forgetting the fee He paid was paid for me too,

and i have a price, and cost, and responsibility in that identity.

every day He's showing me that these chains are heavy but not forever,

He's helping me break free.

marlo afton was born on the eighth of november, 2003. she's currently living her dreams attending school at brigham young university and obtaining a degree in entrepreneurial management. she loves everything art, writing, and how words capture memories and hold feelings that are hard to express out loud. when marlo's not daydreaming, writing, or listening to music and nature, she's probably with her awesome family. "songs i'd sing." is her first collection of poetry. if you want to hear more, follow her instagram account, @songsiwouldsing.